Philip Venzke

CHANT TO SAVE THE WORLD

SurVision Books

First published in 2022 by
SurVision Books
Dublin, Ireland
Reggio di Calabria, Italy
www.survisionmagazine.com

Copyright © Philip Venzke, 2022
Cover image © Sam Hochstettler, 2022
Design © SurVision Books, 2022

ISBN: 978-1-912963-35-5

This book is in copyright. No part of this publication may be reproduced, stored in a retrieval system, or transmitted in any form or by any means without the prior permission in writing from the publisher.

Acknowledgments

Grateful acknowledgment is made to the editors of the following, in which some of these poems, or versions of them, originally appeared:

Abraxas: "Spelunking"

Barney Street: "Vis-A-Vis" and "Three Views on Baldness"

Clockwise Cat: "The Milk Cemetery"

Gorey Details (3): "Harbor House Pier"

Illumen: "The Eyelash Factory"

Litterbox Magazine: "2:53 A.M."

L'Oeuvre: "Chant to Save the World"

The Legendary: "Make No Bones About It"

The Madison Review: "The Song of the Water Witcher" [with the exception of Part 5]

NOTA (None Of The Above): "Our Baby's First Plane Ride"

Opaque to Radiant (Volume 2): "Nude Reclining on A Stairway," "Dangerous Footprints," and "The Mirror Hears Its Voice"

Right Hand Pointing: "Silence Is Golden"

Sheepshead Review: "Black Zipper"

Song 6: "Wrapped Up In Morning"

SurVision: "Odor of Sanctity"

Verse Wisconsin: "Send Shivers Up Your Spine," "Wild Oats," "Brautigan's Angel," and "Rock Bottom"

CONTENTS

Wrapped Up in Morning	5
The Eyelash Factory	6
The Failure	7
Black Zipper	8
Chant to Save the World	9
Three Views on Baldness	10
Vis-A-Vis	12
Spelunking	13
The Mirror Hears Its Voice	14
Our Baby's First Plane Ride	16
Nude Reclining on a Stairway	17
Odor of Sanctity	18
Dangerous Footprints	19
Doctor, I Can Hear My Eyes!	20
Silence Is Golden	21
Brautigan's Angel	22
The Milk Cemetery	24
Wild Oats	25
Rock Bottom	26
Make No Bones About It	28
Send Shivers Up Your Spine	29
The Song of the Water Witcher	30
2:53 A.M.	35
Harbor House Pier	36

Wrapped Up in Morning

Ushering us in, the hostess sat me
in the peanut gallery of Hell, and
said, "No Remarks". Quetzalcoatl and three
angels penetrated the unopened
curtain, did a loop-the-loop, and landed
atop the apex of the largest licorice
column. Cortez snickered behind me. Ice-
cream made Sistine designs on his beard, as
nude women with peyote buttons as
pasties savored the magnificent prize.../

/Adsum! Thru the half-mirror, down toward
the street, I see children bending by Fords.
The night got the asphalt drunk again last
night; it puked up worms and swore a fast.

The Eyelash Factory

Thank you for the eyelash.
It arrived in today's mail.
I don't want to sound ungrateful
but you forgot to tell me
how to use the eyelash.
The cat said I should blow it off
my fingertip and make a wish.
But recent events have shown
that eyelashes tend to burst
into dust if stared at too long.
Please don't get upset,
but I'd like more eyelashes.
I know one should be my limit,
but you see I've taken up seeing.
This is no joke. My room will soon
be wallpapered with eyes.
Eyes looking left and right.
Eyes looking up and down.
Eyes staring straight ahead.
So, please ask your factory
to quadruple the production,
then expedite the order promptly.
The eyeballs above my bed
have been complaining lately
about wanting to wink.

The Failure

The more he fails,
the more he tries.
He falls short,
but keeps on trying.
He starts construction,
but loses the blueprints.
He buys "how-to" books,
but the instructions are missing.
He collects second-hand medals
hoping that they will breed.
If any of these succeed,
he fails to notice.
Even his sleep
is not up to snuff.
One dream thrives:
He is running,
and is first
across the finish line,
looking down
to find no feet.

Black Zipper

Now a frost
fills our teeth.
It makes us brittle,
this blood colored
stitching
sewed to our backs.

Complex stitching
shaped by
a thousand waiting needles.

And an infinite weight
clings to the clasp.
And a fifth frozen hand
sleeps in the nest of our past.

Too soon we will begin to love
the fabric that tugs at our backs.
And in the naked womb
a forgotten zipper
madly tries to close.

Chant to Save the World

Mau, mau,
Boo, boo,
Ox, gob,
Nurb, murble,
Eye, yie,
Yippie, yie, yea

Three Views on Baldness

1.

My grandfather
no longer dreams of hair

no longer watches hair
Instead he watches the lawn

Each night the lawn grows
thicker and shorter

In his dreams he knows only this
he has more and more face to wash

2.

I dream of women's hair

Hair that grows from the lawn
up to the white heads of statues

Each night the hair adds more
and more light to the moon

I watch the hair grow dark
and thick enough to bite

3.

My father dreams of hair

He watches his hair falling
onto the grass in the backyard

Each night the lawn is filled
deeper and deeper with hair

Soon he will wade across the lawn
the sea of hair parting around him

Vis-A-Vis

There is a scar
in the air
behind my body
that only your scar
can touch.
It is a wound,
a flaw that hides
feathers on fire.
When we stand
back to back
in the sun
our bodies turn
into bright wings.

Spelunking

Standing on the edge of her ear
I look into the dark opening
and lay down my rope
and blow out my light.

Removing my clothing
I grasp a hair
and swing in
toward my death.

The Mirror Hears Its Voice

And the plums roll back up the tree
and slam back onto the stem

And the trees bark down at the lawn of hand mirrors
and the silver glass is shattered

And slivers fly up and slice off clouds
and leave open sores in the sky

And the plum trees cough down bloody phlegm
and car tires are glued to the street

And the last cat in town is stitched
and sewn to the only working car motor

And the fruitless wombs of mature adults burst open
and crows fly out carrying human hearts in their beaks

And they fly backwards into the open sores in the sky
and they cry: love, love, love

And the clouds bounce back into the sky
and stuff shut the sores

And hand mirrors sprout on the lawn
and cats carry smiling fish heads

And the fish heads smile back at the hand mirrors
And the hand mirrors smile back

And bark

Our Baby's First Plane Ride

You squeezed through the window
and out onto the wing
and crawled,
never afraid,
because to you the wing is covered in sticky tar.
At the wing's tip you lie down
on your naked back,
tar fingering into your pores.
Your featherless arms pull the plane along
each time you grasp a cloud.
And the wind pushes into your ears
and caterwauls out your mouth.
No one
can ever come out to get you,
and the plane will never land
while your weight is on the wing.
And you cry,
and press yourself down
hard into the tar;
wanting the sun
to seal the tar around you,
wanting the sun
to bleach your bones,
wanting the sun
to iron shut your eyes.

Nude Reclining on a Stairway

1.

The bottom step is pink.
A beaver is biting a pot of honey.
Its fur is wet and slick
And someone has stolen the spoon.

2.

The next step is white.
A pencil eraser is nailed down through a silver dollar
And into half of a muskmelon.
Another eraser nails down a tangerine.

3.

The third step is red.
A pistol sleeps on a butterfly.
Its barrel is aimed at the moon.
A bullet is halfway there.

Odor of Sanctity

There is an obscene elephant
rotting in the living room corner
and we keep bumping into it.
Seems it was a wedding present
that we were afraid to open.
Now it's too late to return it.
We find shells under our pillows
and footprints in our butter.
Our toilet smells of peanuts.
Blind men circle our house.
When epileptic pygmies
are seen arriving after midnight,
we bring in a shaman for aid.
He puts lipstick on clam shells
until coconuts burp from the ceiling
and parrots fart from the walls.
Nothing works. The decay continues.
After the shaman leaves, we amble,
from room to room, turning off lights.
When the night light flickers out,
we hear a snicker.

Dangerous Footprints

The slugs in the garden
decide
with bunions
with corns
with ingrown toenails
to walk
down her cheeks
and the slowness
at which this decision is executed
is so exhausting
that no one notices
the upside down
half buried
derailed locomotive
lying with the tomatoes.

Doctor, I Can Hear My Eyes!

(The Hyperacusis Lament)

Every "S" has a rancid smell
like a lyme scratching its ear
or a snake bending its tail
to remove some earwax.
The mosquito snores,
the eyelash sighs,
the fruit fly whispers,
and the leaf sneezes.
O Tullio, Tullio
where for art thou Tullio?
Your phenomenon sucks!
Try to hide in the basement,
but spider webs whistle,
mouse traps wheeze,
the joists crack and ache
and when you squeeze
your eyes real tight
you can hear your brain ring.
Get Ophelia's hand
off the volume knob!
Something rumbles overhead
must be my hair clicking its heels...
I am an ear of corn
each kernel popping
into a stethoscope.

Silence Is Golden

"When I kept silent, my bones wasted away."
—Psalm 32:3

he kept silent she kept silent
they didn't hear each other

who is who no one knows

their tongues are strangers
they have marrow for meals

no one can find their bones

the ground begins to yawn
it has nothing to say

Brautigan's Angel

*"In the fourth inning
an angel committed
suicide by jumping
off a low cloud."*
—Richard Brautigan

After eons
of taking orders
from archangels,
principalities, powers,
virtues, dominions,
thrones, cherubim,
and seraphim;
and after millennia
of delivering messages
no one wanted to hear;
and after centuries
of trying to find
any goodness to reward;
and after decades
of punishing
never ending injustice;
he came home exhausted
only to find his clouds
had been re-arranged.
The ball game
had already started.
And his father-in-law

was lounging
in *his* favorite cloud.
Later, near the end
of a double play,
sulking for innings
on a low cloud,
he finally spoke up:
*"You had no right.
Please apologize."*
Then his father-in-law
leaned down from his cloud
and from that open grave
of a throat droned:
"You ain't no angel either."

The Milk Cemetery

Lactose became so intolerant
of bovines that it took out
its distress on by-products.
Yogurt was kidnapped,
whey was high jacked,
curds were given wedgies,
and cheese was tied up naked
in a girl's locker room.
Gangs of soy beans
soon owned the streets.
They jostled shops serving latte.
They roughed up waffle cones.
They barked at ice cream vendors.
Soon milk spin-offs became illicit
and speakcheesies colonized dark alleys.
Blind cats listened for the secret knock.
And everyone knew that *The Churn*
had the best rhythm in town.
When the bribes of butter
couldn't keep the cops at bay,
the raids milked several concerns.
Pints, quarts, and gallons
were poured out in the street.
How the moon shined on that puddle.
But in a secret, hidden barn
cows continued to package powdered milk.
People didn't care that it was skimmed.

Wild Oats

A packet of wild oats,
wearing leather jackets,
saunter into town.

*"We ain't looking for
no trouble,"* they state.

They snap open
switchblades and slice
trenches in the dirt.

Their merrymaking
lasts only a minute
and disturbs no one.

First light finds them
lodged in the ground.

The sheriff declares:
*"That's some sowing
they did last night."*

Despondent, he loads
his pistol with blanks.

Rock Bottom

"If they keep quiet, the stones will cry out."
—Luke 19:40

Stones
began to blister the ground,
the day after tongues
melted around molars.
Now ignoring gravity's hand,
gritty stones burrow up,
swim under streams,
dance around mountains,
tread over oceans,
and unearth each other
until no pebble is left unturned.
There are poignant nods
as they congregate together
and discuss their calling.
Then, from the muck of an empty well
a lone stone begins to caterwaul.
Just a boulder's throw away
a wall joins in the wailing.
Then an avalanche connects,
a pile unites, a pathway bonds
until a glass house shudders.
Sticks beg to marry stones.
They dream of their offspring:
great bone breakers.

When stone walls
keep getting in the way,
the search intensifies
to find out who cast the first stone.

Make No Bones About It

"I can count all my bones; people stare and gloat over me."
—Psalm 22:17

After they were done staring,
they said: "Are you done?
We have about 206 bones to pick with you.
Get up you bag of bones.
We said get up. Get up.
Don't you have a bone in your body?"
I said: "Please let me explain."
I pleaded: "I know how it all started."
I told them: "In the beginning,
there was one bone.
Some wanted it named: cut to the.
Others wanted it named: chilled to the.
While others wanted: bad to the.
That argument had no end.
One bone snapped into two bones.
Two bones broke into four bones.
Until a pile of bones remained:
mean, jealous, unkind bones."
They hated my bare boned story.
When they returned
they brought sticks and stones.
I had no defense –
I had misplaced my funny bone.

Send Shivers Up Your Spine

By mistake, a wild vertebrae,
raised by a pack of wolves,
wandered into a movie theater.

Soon it is surrounded
by boxes of hot buttered
popcorn madly throwing goobers.

Now anchored against the stage,
keystones grab pitch forks
and lynchpins light torches.

The crowd taunts and chants:
"Why don't you get a backbone?"
The ignorant bone cowers
under a chair, spineless.

The Song of the Water Witcher

1.

born
under a willow tree
I stretch my arms
and cry

a white pebble
rolls out of my mouth
and into a stream

it feels its weight
as it sinks
and it sings a song

I curl my toes
and smile

2.

crawling on a hilltop
my knees press onto a white pebble

I sit and send it rolling downhill

it gathers speed and becomes larger

it knocks down trees and leaves a widening path

I lose sight of it as it rolls into the plain

at hills base a stream calls out my name
and I press my knees over my ears

soon I am rolling down the hill

3.

where ever I walk
a white pebble follows me
through a maze of underground streams

everyday I listen to it sing its song

it teaches me how to carve a flute
from a willow branch
dry it in the sun for three days
and play the song it taught

at night I play that song
under a willow tree
and watch the leaves shudder

4.

I went to a willow tree
because a fire was in my hands
and I cut and peeled a willow stick
and tied to one end a string

on the other end I made a loop
and when the moon was full and white
I cast the loop onto the moon
and tugged and pulled it down

I dipped the moon into a stream
to drown the water's voice
I pressed the moon inside my hands
and squeezed it down to size

I buried the white pebble
beneath a willow tree
and at night I climb and sit
and listen to the pebble cry

5.

Call me plumber
I have captured water
I can control her
I dig wells down to her and pump her up
   from where she is hiding
I can soften her if she is hard
I can warm her if she is cold
I can send her through a maze of pipes
I can send her cold half through a thick pipe
   to make her move slower
I can send her warm half through a thin pipe
   to bring her to me quicker
I can bring both halves together

I can make her wash my hands and feet
   and my clothes and my food and I watch
   her choke on dirt
I can make her sing throughout the house
   and when I run my hand along any wall
   I can feel her softly tapping
I am the only one who can make her bubble
   forth in a stream
I am the only one who can make her
   suddenly stop

6.

I must journey across a desert
I must follow an empty stream bed
I must find the source of the stream

I listen to moths tap their wings together
to help me remember the sound of water

I lean on a crooked willow stick
to help me in walking

I suck on a white pebble
to fight against thirst

7.

The source of the stream is a bottomless lake

I drop my white pebble and watch it sink

the music of the water wearing away its body
haunts my pebble

as it becomes a last white speck
it sings its last song to me

and for the rest of my life
I must carry pebbles in my mouth
and listen to my voice rumble

and for the rest of my life
I must listen to the sound a stone
exudes as it begins to crack

and for the rest of my life
I must feel the willow's bark
twist and break in my hands
as it bends down to water

2:53 A.M.

Each and every night
this piece of time
disembarks my sleep.
Now, this isn't just any minute.
In fact, this moment has a job.
Indeed, it has made a career
of reminding me nightly
of what I would like to forget.
It begins its work quickly.
That second hand squanders
none of those sixty clicks
as it dances on the clock,
glad-hands the mirror,
schmooze's the moon,
and high-five's a shadow
prowling in a corner.
And when the work is done,
the time card is punched.
Without wasting a second,
it grabs the empty lunch pail
and, in the rain, heads to the bar.
Most of the two o'clock crew
are already there and cavorting.
All night long their loud reminiscing
ticks, ticks, ticks in my head.

Harbor House Pier

The wind drags its breath
in and out

Waves show us teeth

The red moon pales

We race back
back into the throat of night

Selected Poetry Titles Published by SurVision Books

Seeds of Gravity: An Anthology of Contemporary Surrealist Poetry from Ireland
Edited by Anatoly Kudryavitsky
ISBN 978-1-912963-18-8

Invasion: An Anthology of Ukrainian Poetry about the War
Edited by Tony Kitt
ISBN 978-1-912963-32-4

Noelle Kocot. *Humanity*
(New Poetics: USA)
ISBN 978-1-9995903-0-7

Marc Vincenz. *Einstein Fledermaus*
(New Poetics: USA)
ISBN 978-1-912963-20-1

Helen Ivory. *Maps of the Abandoned City*
(New Poetics: England)
ISBN 978-1-912963-04-1

Tony Kitt. *The Magic Phlute*
(New Poetics: Ireland)
ISBN 978-1-912963-08-9

Clayre Benzadón. *Liminal Zenith*
(New Poetics: USA)
ISBN 978-1-912963-11-9

Thomas Townsley. *Tangent of Ardency*
(New Poetics: USA)
ISBN 978-1-912963-15-7

Anton Yakovlev. *Chronos Dines Alone*
(Winner of James Tate Poetry Prize 2018)
ISBN 978-1-912963-01-0

Mikko Harvey & Jake Bauer. *Idaho Falls*
(Winner of James Tate Poetry Prize 2018)
ISBN 978-1-912963-02-7

John Bradley. *Spontaneous Mummification*
(Winner of James Tate Poetry Prize 2019)
ISBN 978-1-912963-13-3

John Thomas Allen. *Rolling in the Third Eye*
(Winner of James Tate Poetry Prize 2019)
ISBN 978-1-912963-15-7

Gary Glauber. *The Covalence of Equanimity*
(Winner of James Tate Poetry Prize 2019)
ISBN 978-1-912963-12-6

Charles Kell. *Pierre Mask*
(Winner of James Tate Poetry Prize 2019)
ISBN 978-1-912963-19-5

Charles Borkhuis. *Spontaneous Combustion*
(Winner of James Tate Poetry Prize 2021)
ISBN 978-1-912963-30-0

George Kalamaras. *That Moment of Wept*
ISBN 978-1-9995903-7-6

George Kalamaras. *Through the Silk-Heavy Rains*
ISBN 978-1-912963-28-7

Order our books from http://survisionmagazine.com/bookshop.htm

www.ingramcontent.com/pod-product-compliance
Lightning Source LLC
Chambersburg PA
CBHW061312040426
42444CB00010B/2604